You Can't Eat MY Foot!

By David Doucette

For any questions about usage or to contact the author, please contact Douce572@yahoo.com.

First Edition.

ISBN 978-1-0881-6606-2

This is a work of fiction. While based on a true story, it is in fact loosely based on a true story. Creative liberties are in abundance. Any likeness of all fun-loving characters, characterization, locations and pictures are purely coincidental.

Written and created by
David Doucette

Dedicated to my inspiration, Eve, who showed me that the difficulty of being a father can also be so rewarding.

And to my strength, Danielle, for your support and love in all I do.

To my readers - I cannot thank you enough for giving "You Can't Eat MY Foot!" a chance. I hope you find as much joy reading it as I did in creating it.

Based on a True Story...
Inspired by a Father's Love.

It all started one day when
I realized....

I could reach my FOOT!

And, not only could I reach it...

I could eat it!

That was the day my entire life changed....

I mean, a lot!

But, this time was different.

You see, I was very aware...

That I was just a lil person!

And then, my biggest fear came true!

One of the big people tried to eat my foot!

I mean, it is one thing if I want to eat my own foot.

But who did he think he was to eat somebody else's foot?!

I tried to stop him, believe me.

But remember, lil person, so size was not on my side.

"It is mine!" I screamed and cried...

"You Can't Eat My Foot!"

But they just sat there and did nothing!

I tried everything…

Even pretending to sleep.

But even then, big people ate my foot!

I was beginning to lose hope.

Then, I realized I might not actually be saying…

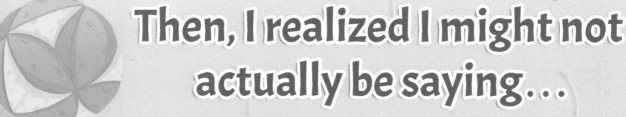

"You can't eat my foot!"

How did I know, you ask?

Well, I thought foot was said "googoogaga."

But when the big people held up my foot, they said...

"Can I eat your F O O T?"

Well, right there a light bulb went off!

The big people just didn't understand me!

So, I set out to do some research...

It turns out, foot is hard to say for lil people!

But do you know what's easy to say?

And when the big people tried to eat my foot...

I said it loud and proud!

NO, NO, NO, NO, NO, and NO!

They stopped eating my foot!

So, listen up all my lil people out there.

Don't ever think you don't have a voice!

Because you do!

Look at me.

I still have my feet!

Yes, I was a lil person.

But I wasn't afraid to speak up!

This lil person's the Boss of me!

Printed in the USA
CPSIA information can be obtained
at www.ICGtesting.com
LVHW051315091223
765940LV00013B/1010